The First Christmas

Written by ANITA GANERI

Illustrated by MAGGIE DOWNER

Derrydale Books

New York/Avenel, New Jersey

A TEMPLAR BOOK

This 1992 edition published by Derrydale Books,
distributed by Outlet Book Company, Inc., a Random House Company,
40 Engelhard Avenue, Avenel, New Jersey 07001.

Devised and produced by The Templar Company plc,
Pippbrook Mill, London Road, Dorking, Surrey RH4 1JE, Great Britain.

Edited by Wendy Madgwick
Designed by Janie Louise Hunt
Printed and bound in Singapore

ISBN 0-517-06971-7
8 7 6 5 4 3 2 1

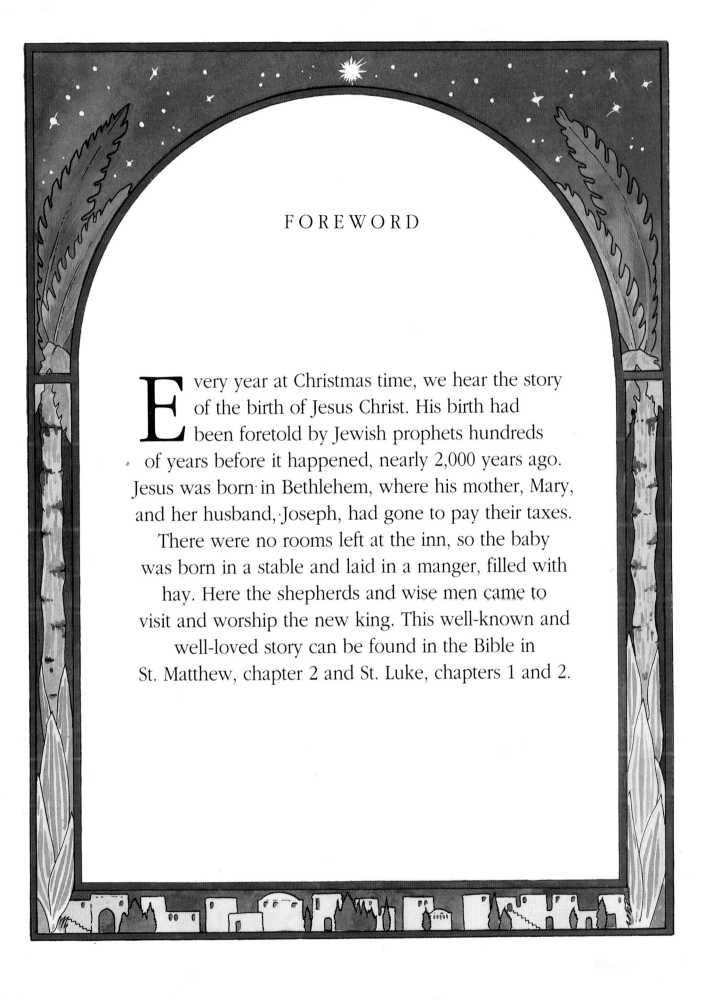

FOREWORD

Every year at Christmas time, we hear the story of the birth of Jesus Christ. His birth had been foretold by Jewish prophets hundreds of years before it happened, nearly 2,000 years ago. Jesus was born in Bethlehem, where his mother, Mary, and her husband, Joseph, had gone to pay their taxes. There were no rooms left at the inn, so the baby was born in a stable and laid in a manger, filled with hay. Here the shepherds and wise men came to visit and worship the new king. This well-known and well-loved story can be found in the Bible in St. Matthew, chapter 2 and St. Luke, chapters 1 and 2.

Long, long ago, in the little village of Nazareth in Israel, there lived a young woman called Mary. One day, Mary was busy as usual doing her household chores. She had just swept the floor and was about to start preparing the family's supper when an astonishing thing happened. The room was filled with a strange, bright light, and Mary heard a soft voice calling her name.

Startled, she looked around. A shining figure—the Angel Gabriel—appeared before her. Alarmed, Mary took a step backwards, raising a hand to shield her eyes against the light.

"The Lord is with you, Mary," Gabriel said. "He is very pleased with you and has chosen you for a special purpose. You will soon have a baby boy, who will be called Jesus. He will be the Son of God, and will save the world from wickedness and bad deeds."

Mary was frightened and confused. She did not understand how such a thing could happen. But the angel was gentle and kind.

"Fear not," he said, "with God all things are possible." Trembling, Mary looked up at Gabriel.

"I am the Lord's servant," she said quietly. "I will obey him whatever he tells me to do." Then Gabriel disappeared, leaving Mary alone in the room to ponder on the news the angel had brought to her.

Mary was engaged to be married to a man called Joseph, the village carpenter. She was worried about telling him her news. Quietly Mary explained to him what the Angel had said and that she was going to have a baby. At first, Joseph was unhappy. He did not understand why God had chosen Mary and did not know whether they should still get married.

"I wish I knew what to do," he thought.

That night, when Joseph was fast asleep, he had a strange dream. The Angel Gabriel appeared in front of him saying,

"You have nothing to fear, Joseph. There is no need for you to worry. Mary's baby is very special, but he will still need your love and help. You will be like his father. Go ahead and marry Mary, she will be a good wife and you will be happy. You, too, will be doing what God wants."

So Mary and Joseph got married and settled down to a happy life together. Joseph continued with his carpentry work, while Mary looked after their house and their few goats and sheep.

One day, a few months later, Joseph came back home bursting with important news for Mary. At that time, the Romans ruled the country, and Roman soldiers were everywhere. They kept the peace and made sure that the instructions of their emperor, Caesar Augustus, were carried out.

"Whatever has happened?" Mary exclaimed when she saw Joseph hurrying towards their house. He looked excited and annoyed all at the same time.

"Caesar Augustus has sent out an order," panted Joseph. "He wants everyone in the country to go to the town where they were born. We've got to be counted and put on a register so that we can all be taxed." Joseph frowned and shook his head. "What are we doing to do, Mary?" he said. "We will have to go to Bethlehem, where I was born. But it is a long journey to undertake so near to the birth of the child."

Joseph was right. Bethlehem was a long way away from Nazareth and it would take them several days to get there. Joseph was looking forward to seeing his birthplace again, of course, but he was worried that the journey would be too tiring for Mary. Mary tried to put his mind at rest by pointing out that she could ride on one of their donkeys. At least that should not be too tiring for her.

"Don't worry about me," she said. "God will look after us, Joseph. And we cannot disobey the Romans, can we?" Joseph had to agree.

So, the next day, Mary and Joseph packed up their things, and set off, with Mary riding on their little gray donkey.

The road to Bethlehem was rocky, bumpy, and pitted with pot holes. The little donkey did its best not to trip or jolt Mary, but nevertheless it was a very uncomfortable and tiring journey. Luckily, there were lots of other travelers on the road, so they had plenty of people to talk to. Joseph was always happy to swop stories and memories with anyone who had been born in Bethlehem, like him! At night, the weary travelers set up their makeshift camps by the roadside.

They lit fires to keep themselves warm and to scare away wild animals. They cooked a simple supper, then went to sleep on the ground, covered in blankets.

One morning, Joseph, sure that he recognized the countryside, decided to go on ahead to see what lay before them on the road. He had only been gone for a minute or two, when Mary heard him cry out,

"Look! Look! There it is, over there!"

Mary shaded her eyes from the sun and looked to where Joseph was pointing. There in the distance, on the top of a hill, stood a city. It was Bethlehem at last. Mary was very relieved.

"Oh, Joseph, I'll be so glad when we get there."
She took Joseph's arm and gazed at the distant town.
"Our baby son will be born in Bethlehem," she said
softly. "Just like you."

"Yes," Joseph replied, smiling at his wife.
"King David was born in Bethlehem, too. Now
another king will be born there, as the prophets told
us. Let's hurry and get ourselves settled into a nice,
comfy inn! You must get some rest."

So, Mary and Joseph arrived in Bethlehem.
They were tired, aching, and dusty after their long
journey. But the streets were crowded with travelers
who were just as tired as they were. They had come
from far and wide on the orders of the Emperor and
were all looking for somewhere to spend the night.
Mary and Joseph trudged from one inn to another

searching for somewhere to stay. But the inns were all full—there wasn't a spare room to be found anywhere. Everywhere they went, they were told the same thing, "Sorry, no room here!"

"What shall we do, Joseph?" Mary asked. She was tired out and worried. The baby could arrive any time now.

"We'll just try this last inn," Joseph replied, pointing to a welcoming open door. "After that, I really don't know what we'll do."

He knocked wearily on the inn door. The plump, kindly innkeeper bustled up, shaking his head.

"Sorry, we've no more room here."

"Please," Joseph begged. "It is almost time for my wife to have her baby. We will take anything—anything."

"Well now," said the innkeeper, pulling his beard thoughtfully. "Let's see. There's no room in my inn. It's jampacked with folk. But you could use the stable out back. It's not very luxurious, but it's clean and warm. And the cows won't bother you. What do you say?"

Joseph glanced at Mary. She looked so pale and tired.

"Thank you," he said. "We'd be glad of a place to sleep, wherever it is."

The innkeeper picked up a lantern and led them outside to a yard at the back of the inn. There, they found a small stable, filled with the sound of animals patiently chewing their hay. A cow nuzzled

Mary's hand as she bent to stroke its calf. Chickens scratched around the door and a cat purred amongst a pile of sacks.

"We shall be happy here," said Mary.

And so, later that night, in a small stable in the middle of Bethlehem, Jesus, the Son of God, was born. Mary, his mother, wrapped him up snugly in a white, linen blanket and laid him in the manger, filled with soft, warm hay.

Now, on a hillside, just outside the city, a
group of shepherds kept watch over their flock of
sheep. It was a still, quiet night and hardly a sound
could be heard on the dark hillside. Suddenly, the sky
was filled with a marvelous, shining light. An angel,
brighter than the brightest star, appeared in front of
the shepherds. The shepherds were wide awake now
and terrified. They fell on the ground and covered
their eyes, hoping that whatever it was would go away
and leave them alone. But the angel told them that
there was no need to be afraid.

"I have brought good news for you and for everyone on earth," he said, in a beautiful musical voice. "Jesus, the savior, has been born tonight in Bethlehem. You will find him in a stable, lying in a manger of hay. Hurry now and see your new king! Rejoice! Rejoice and be happy!"

Then the angel was joined by hundreds of other angels, all as bright as he was. They filled the dark sky with their singing:

Glory to God in the highest,
and on earth peace,
good will toward men.

It was the sweetest sound the shepherds had ever heard. They wanted it to go on for ever. But as quickly as they had come, the angels suddenly disappeared. For a moment, the shepherds stood with their mouths wide open. They were too amazed to speak or move. Then they all started speaking at once.

"We must go at once and worship Jesus," one of them said.

"Yes! Yes! Let's go," the others agreed.

"But we must take something for him, and we
haven't got anything to give," said another in dismay.
"We haven't got any money or costly treasures."

"We'll take a lamb," the first shepherd said.
"He'll like that. I'm sure he will."

So the shepherds hurried off, with one of them
carrying a tiny, bleating lamb in his arms.

When they reached the stable, they hesitated,
not wanting to disturb Mary and the sleeping child.

"We have brought a gift for the new king," murmured one.

"May we see him?" asked another.

Mary looked up at the shepherds in surprise.

"Who told you?" she asked.

"An angel appeared to us," they explained.

Smiling, Mary nodded and beckoned the shepherds in.

They crowded in, trying to be as quiet as possible. They gave the lamb to Mary to keep safe, and knelt down by the manger to worship the baby and praise God.

Then the shepherds hurried away to tend their sheep. But on their way back, they spread the news far and wide, telling everyone of the amazing sights they had seen and that a new king had been born.

Far, far away, in the east, three wise men were traveling on their camels. They were dressed in rich robes and silk, and had golden rings with precious gems on their fingers. A few days before, the wise men had seen a great star in the sky, shining brightly above them.

"It is the sign we've been waiting for," they said. "The sign that a new king has been born. The star will guide us to him."

So the wise men had set off to find Jesus. They thought that a king would be born in a royal palace and as the nearest royal palace was in Jerusalem, they made their way there.

When the wise men reached the city they asked everyone they met about the new king and where they could find him. But no one seemed to know anything about a new king. The baby was nowhere to be found.

When Herod the King of Judaea heard about
the three wise men he was worried. He called his
priests and asked them where the Christ was to be born.
The priests consulted among themselves and looked at
the ancient scriptures. Then one of them said,

"The prophets said that a king would be born
in Bethlehem, the city of King David."

Herod summoned the wise men. He told them what his priests had said and asked the wise men to return and tell them where the baby could be found so that he, too, could worship him.

So the wise men got back on their camels, and set off again. They slept during the day and traveled at night. Then they could see the star which would lead them to Jesus. At last they reached Bethlehem. The star seemed to come to a halt and hovered above a building—a tiny stable.

The wise men could not believe that this was the place they had been searching for. Why, they could even hear cattle mooing! And yet the whole stable seemed to glow with a heavenly light, so the wise men peeped inside. There they found Mary and Joseph with the baby Jesus. The wise men fell to their knees in front of the manger to worship Jesus. They were full of joy to see his sweet face. Then they

opened up the gifts they had brought with them.

"I bring you gold," said one. "A royal gift fit for a king."

"Sweet-smelling frankincense is my gift," said the second, "because you are holy."

"Myrrh, for the healing of wounds and hurts, I give to you," said the third as he placed his precious gift on the ground.

That night, as they slept, the wise men had a
strange dream. An angel visited them warning them
not to return to Herod's palace as he wanted to harm
the newborn king. Next morning they were amazed to
find they had all had the same dream. They agreed
that they would not risk going to Jerusalem but would
return home by a different route.

But first they decided to pay a final visit to the
new king. They made their way to the stable in the
early morning light. The shepherds, too, had returned
and quietly they all entered the stable, gathering
around the manger.

Overcome with joy, they knelt and worshiped the baby Jesus, giving thanks to God for the birth of their Savior. As they did so, the little stable was filled with a shining light and a host of angels appeared singing and praising God in the highest. And in the middle of them all, sleeping peacefully in His manger, lay the baby Jesus, who had come to save the world from evil.

And that is the story of that very special first Christmas night, many, many years ago, when Jesus was born in Bethlehem. He was not born in a grand palace but in a simple stable, where the innkeeper's cows usually lived. He came not to wear fine clothes and a gold crown, but to save us all and lead us to a better life.

Can you sing the carol which was written to celebrate his birthday and which children everywhere know and love?

Away in a manger, no crib for a bed,
The little Lord Jesus laid down his sweet head;
The stars in the bright sky looked down where he lay,
The little Lord Jesus asleep on the hay.

The cattle are lowing, the baby awakes,
But little Lord Jesus, no crying he makes;
I love thee, Lord Jesus; look down from the sky,
And stay by my side until morning is nigh.

Be near me, Lord Jesus; I ask thee to stay
Close by me for ever, and love me, I pray;
Bless all the dear children in thy tender care,
And fit us for heaven to live with thee there.